Holy Curveballs: Embracing God's Strange Invitations

Holy Curveballs: Embracing God's Strange Invitations

Sermons for the Season After Pentecost (Second Half) Based on the Gospel Lessons for Cycle A

Mary Austin

CSS Publishing Company
Lima, Ohio

FIRST EDITION
Copyright © 2025 by
CSS Publishing Company, Inc.

Library of Congress Cataloging-in-Publication Data
Names: Austin, Mary, 1954- author
Title: Holy curveballs : embracing God's strange invitations : sermons for
 the season after Pentecost (second half) based on the gospel lessons for
 Cycle A / Mary Austin.
Description: First edition. | Lima, Ohio : CSS Publishing Company, [2025]
Identifiers: LCCN 2025032633 (print) | LCCN 2025032634 (ebook) | ISBN
 9780788031410 paperback | ISBN 9780788031403 adobe pdf
Subjects: LCSH: Pentecost season--Sermons | Bible. Matthew--Sermons |
 Sermons, American--21st century | Common lectionary (1992). Year A
Classification: LCC BV4300.5 .A97 2025 (print) | LCC BV4300.5 (ebook)
LC record available at https://lccn.loc.gov/2025032633
LC ebook record available at https://lccn.loc.gov/2025032634

For more information about CSS Publishing Company resources, vis-it our website at www.csspub.com, email us at csr@csspub.com, or call (800) 241-4056.

e-book:
ISBN-13: 978-0-7880-3140-3
ISBN-10: 0-7880-3140-6

ISBN-13: 978-0-7880-3141-0
ISBN-10: 0-7880-3141-4 PRINTED IN USA

*For the people of First Congregational Church,
Kalamazoo, Michigan, who know how to love God
with energy and laughter.*

Contents

Introduction

Matthew has never been my favorite gospel — until now.

John is poetic, Luke is compassionate, Mark is spare, and Matthew never had a particular flavor, for me, until this year. Spending time with Matthew, made me admire how protective he is of his community of believers. As he tells the story of Jesus, he's a fierce sheepdog, guarding his flock from any hint that they are inferior to other believers. He fends off any idea that their faith is less than anyone else's. As he connects the story of Jesus to the faith of Israel, Matthew also makes room for newcomers.

This is welcome news for us, since all of us are newcomers to the way of Jesus.

Matthew has another lesson to offer — he isn't afraid to wade into controversy, which is useful these days. If you were raised to be a nice kind of Christian, Matthew offers us the gift of fierce faith. Reading through his gospel amps up the courage of our convictions.

Spending time with Matthew for the last few months has been a gift to my faith, and I hope that you and your congregation receive this same gift from Matthew, as his gospel guides you through this season.

Blessings to you and your unique community of faith,
Mary Austin

If Peter Gets It Wrong, Can We Ever Get It Right?

One summer, my brother and I lined up our schedules to visit our dad at the same time. We thought it would be fun to be there together. We arrived for our week of planned movies and ice cream to find our dad in the hospital, with no sign of getting out. Each day, the doctors came in and hemmed and hawed, pondering possibilities out loud, never quite sure of the path they wanted to take, never settling on any course of action, always promising to come back the next day.

Finally, trying to read the tea leaves, I asked them, "Is hospice a possibility?"

"Oh, yes," they said, with evident relief. "We can make that happen today." They zipped off to order equipment, write orders, schedule transportation, and my dad was home that afternoon.

It always intrigues me how fast things move when you're having the right conversation.

* * *

In this text, Peter was reluctant to enter into that conversation.

Just before this, Jesus had been tested by rival religious groups, and then Peter declared that Jesus was the Messiah. In a moment of revelation, Jesus asked the disciples what people were saying about him. They told him that people were suggesting his late cousin John, or the great prophet Elijah, or others. Then he asked the key question: "What do you all say? You know me best." Peter, with his characteristic energy, jumped in with the answer. "You are the Messiah, the Son of the living God." For that answer, Jesus offered him a blessing, and a place in the coming reign of God.

After this, people longing for a Messiah might expect a detailed plan for overthrowing the Romans, plus instructions about getting rid of all those soldiers who were conducting a reign of terror in their country. His plan for an end to foreign rule. Nope. Instead, Jesus continued on, in this passage, to adjust their hopes. Or, as a leader in my church often says, "manage expectations."

After that big letdown, Peter wasn't so eager, and who can blame him? A minute ago, he was the rock of a new community, and the holder of the keys. Now all of that power was vanishing, and reality was back. Whatever they were expecting, Jesus said it was going to end in suffering and death. Assuredly his and most probably theirs.

What happened to all that glory and power that Peter was imagining?

We can see why he's so disappointed by the way Jesus describes the reign of God.

Many days, we're disappointed, too.

We would love for God to come in power. We would rejoice to see an end to systemic poverty, racism, and homophobia. We would love to see God end all the conflict in our world, in our schools, in our homes, and even within ourselves. We look forward to the day when no one is abused, battered, or raped ever again. We would love a world free of economic hardship, where no one is sleeping on the street, or working in horrible conditions for low wages.

* * *

On our way there, Jesus said we're not asking the right questions.

We're not having the right conversation.

He asks us the same questions he asked the disciples.

Who do you say that I am?

Can you follow me?

Can you take up your cross — face the burdens of your life, and carry the cares of the world?

As he looked toward his death, Jesus was focused on these questions. He wanted his followers to be pointed in the right direction, so they could keep expanding the love of God after he was gone.

We have questions to ask ourselves, too.

Does our work use the talents God gave us? By work, I mean however we spend our days: raising kids, paid work, volunteer work and the like.

Do our relationships show the love and grace of God? When we talk to our friends, neighbors, partner, and children, are we talking to the face of God in them?

Does the way we use our money reflect our love for God?

Do our lives show evidence of God's presence?

Are we growing in some way, or are we stuck?

What do we regret? How can we not do that anymore?

If we had three months to live, what would we want to fit into our lives?

* * *

One writer [David Goetz in *Death by Suburb*] wrote, "The human tendency seems to be to fight the difficult parts of life, as if by resisting them I can skip to the good stuff or set a few extra goals to overcome the suffering...But there's no entry into Christ's presence without the cross. No one has to go looking for one, the cross finds you."

The cross finds us.

The cross that we pick up is different for each of us — a cross that fits our strength to carry it, and the service that we alone can offer to God. A cross that uses our struggles and heartache to connect us to the hurt of the world, if we can pick it up.

In our different lives, maybe we're picking up the cross of recovery, and a journey of sobriety. Or maybe it's choosing to care for an ill family member, if we have the skills for it. Maybe our work is inclusion, or maybe it's holding on through chemotherapy, and learning a new relationship with our bodies.

13

Maybe it's choosing to work less, and be a better partner, or choosing to get home for family time. Perhaps our cross is the work of anger management or learning to trust. Other times, the cross has no discernible benefit for us. We can choose to serve through a non-profit, or through gifts of money, or through the church.

If we want to follow — and Jesus is clear that we have a choice — this is the path.

This doesn't make us doormats, it makes us people who are willing to have hard conversations and ask the right questions. It makes us people who are willing to use our gifts to make Jesus' vision for the world come alive.

* * *

The questions Jesus asks are our compass through life, pointing us to what really matters to us, signaling us where God would have us go. They are signposts, showing us where we're unhappy...missing something...going too fast...They lead us into the mystery of how we follow God's leading in the places where are, with the gifts we have.

And at the center of it all, there are questions that give meaning to all the others.

Jesus has questions for us, too.

Who do you say that I am?

Can you face your burdens, and care for the needs of others?

When we do, the cross finds us.

When we have the right conversations with God, others and ourselves, the path opens. Step by step, we enter into God's world. All along, God is leading us deeper and deeper into this life of faith.

The cross finds us, and Jesus is there to help us carry it.

With thanks to the God who uses all of us, Amen.

Is Jesus In My Knitting Group?

If someone asked you to describe yourself, what words would you use?

Some things are easy. Parent, partner, sibling. Our friendships and family relationships come to mind first, and so does our work. Teacher, banker, coach. We root ourselves in geography, being proud alums of our high school or college. When you dig even deeper, what else comes to mind? Cyclist, football fan, knitter, artist? Gardener, bowler, trumpet player? Neighbor, PTA member, hospital volunteer?

Those parts of ourselves thrive in groups, where we can talk to other people about our passions. In fact, best-selling author James Clear said, in *Atomic Habits*, that one of the best ways to build good habits is to be part of a group where the habits we want are normal behavior. Want to exercise more? Join a walking group or a yoga class. We get inspired when we see other people eating healthy food, or saving money, or serving lunch at the community center. "Nothing sustains motivation better than belonging to the tribe," he says. In a community, we can take on a whole new identity as volunteers, or tennis players, or tutors.

* * *

In this passage, Jesus was teaching us to be part of a community.

This text and next week's math lesson from Jesus really belong together, as part of the same teaching. Interestingly, only Matthew has these instructions. Those words don't show up in the other gospels.

When the early church told stories about what Jesus said, and wrote down the gospels, they remembered this instruction about how to live with other people in the same community. Matthew's gospel was written down as the early church, the early followers of Jesus, were separating from the Jewish faith. We know this was a time of great upheaval. The great Jerusalem temple had been destroyed. Some people of faith were following Jesus as the Messiah, and others were not. Family members were pulled in different directions. We can feel the pain of family separations, and divisions between neighbors, as their faiths separated from each other. The Jewish faith is long established and has its own norms and rules. This new community of Jesus followers has to figure out how they're going to act. They need to know how to be a community.

The followers of Jesus continued to live in community together. Sometimes, it went well, and the church excelled at loving and supporting people. Other times, we have to keep learning to do better.

And, since then, the church has evolved since then, maybe to a point Jesus wouldn't recognize. Would he understand the words "Property Committee" or "Investment Guidelines" or "Altar Guild"? We have ways of doing ministry and serving God that he couldn't have imagined...and yet this advice remains for us when we disagree with each other.

* * *

How can we do this better?

How can our community be stronger, and more loving?

Clarence Jordan, the founder of the Koinonia Community in Georgia, offered us an example of how to do this. Even when he was a small child, the racial disparities of the South weighed on him. He saw people working hard to barely get by all around him, and he came to believe that poverty was a spiritual problem, as well as an economic one. In college, he got a degree in agriculture, then went to seminary, and then earned a PhD in Greek. In the segregated world of Georgia in the 1950's, he and his wife, Florence, started a small experiment called Koinonia, an intentional community of people who had not very much in common. They were determined to be a place of equality and nonviolence, sharing their land and possessions. Clarence Jordan called it a "demonstration plot for the kingdom of God." They began with three principles: All people are related in God's eyes. Live in accordance with Christ's love. Common ownership—distributing goods and income according to first-century Christian principles based on need, not profit.

Jordan often said, "We haven't gotten anywhere until we see the Word become flesh." He was determined to make that happen, demonstrating how it worked.

During the 1950's, the community flourished, as the Jordans and their neighbors farmed together, studied the Bible, and ate together. The outside world wasn't used to seeing people of color and white people eating together, let alone living together. Their neighbors responded with threats, damage to their farm, and boycotts of their farm products. Their income dropped to almost nothing. In response to the boycotts, Clarence Jordan started a mail order pecan business. Their slogan was "Help us ship the nuts out of Georgia."

Even after experiencing gunfire from neighbors and then being banned from his church, Clarence Jordan somehow managed not to be afraid. He managed to keep his focus on the community, and on ways to grow.

* * *

Jesus invites us into that kind of focus, too.

He calls us to that kind of interaction with our neighbors, our fellow church members, and even our fellow citizens.

Most of us are not peacemakers at the level of Clarence Jordan. Even in our more ordinary lives, peace and connection are still possible. It's hard work, for sure. When we're trying to live with these principles of reconciliation, Jesus said to start with the people close to us. We can practice on the difficult member of our book group, or the annoying person in our friend group.

We can practice on the nitpicky person on our church board, or on the teacher who's always in a bad mood.

* * *

But who deserves our attention?

At first glance, Jesus' instruction seems harsh. If the people with a disagreement can't come to an understanding about what will change, then, he says, let the person in error "be to you as a gentile and a tax collector." Ouch. Are they supposed to be thrown out of the community? Is this a story about harsh discipline?

To our shame, many churches have taken it that way.

But for Jesus, this was a story about reconciliation. It was about wholeness, for the community and for individual people.

For Jesus, tax collectors and Gentiles were the people who needed extra love and attention. He ate dinner with them. He patiently answered their questions. He took time out of his day to heal their children. He assured them of their worth. He loved them, even when they appeared to be unlovable.

Give them more, not less, he was saying. More love, more patience, more care, he said, until people are so overwhelmed with generosity that they change on their own, knowing how beloved they are.

* * *

That last sentence of Jesus' is really interesting.

Where two or three are gathered, he said, he's there, too.

We often take it to mean that powerful things happen in a small worship service, or we can still get work done with a small, determined group. True. That's not all, though.

But, set with these other verses, Jesus was saying that when we do this hard work of speaking the truth, and hearing the truth, he's present in the middle of the effort. When we wade in with someone, all nervous about what to say, he's there in spirit to help us. When we have to hear a hard truth about ourselves, he's there in the conversation to help us learn from it. When we're peeling back the layers of polite conversation, longing to go deeper and be part of a true community, he's there in our trembling efforts. He's in this work that feels so hard. He's part of this process of telling and hearing the truth, that we so often avoid because it's hard. He's in the space between us, as we do the hard work of loving each other.

* * *

A sports team, a knitting group, a class, a workplace — we all belong to different groups. We're part of a family, or our friends who become chosen family. All of these groups are fun and add to our skills and our good habits.

And when you manage to add love, they become a community, even more than a group. When you add honesty, they become a reflection of God's world on earth. Then we're going even deeper with each other. When you add patience and forgiveness, you have a "demonstration plot" for the world of God. Then we have the hope of true growth, and the connection that gives us life.

In the truth of our own lives, Jesus is present, leading us into deeper community. That's where Jesus invites us to live, and to welcome others.

In the spirit of holy community, thanks be to God.

Amen.

Proper 19 (24)
Matthew 18:21-35

Jesus Is A Math Teacher

The writer Anne Lamott famously said that we human beings do things that make Jesus want to drink gin out of the cat bowl.

Well, right back at you, Jesus.

This parable is impossible.

We hear what Jesus said and start to hyperventilate, because it feels so hard. We all have people who are hard to forgive. Our mental math begins. Our minds race with our list of exceptions. Puppy kickers. Crazy family members. Demanding friends. The progressives. The libtards. The conservatives. The gun-lovers. The tree-huggers. Extremists of every kind. Abusers. Those people — whoever they are — who are ruining our country.

Our time is often called the "age of rage."

We are mad about everything.

Even if we don't start the day mad, it's easy to work ourselves up into it, after a few minutes of the news, or a short scroll through social media.

We say things to each other online that we wouldn't say in person, and rage begets more rage. Anger is addictive. We want more and more of it. It has its own energy, and it gives us the illusion of power. When we all feel so powerless, anger is a way out. The first servant in the story sees how powerless he is, and he immediately reaches out to restore his power over the next person. We like to shed our bad feelings by passing them on to someone else.

* * *

Like many parables, this one is exaggerated, so we really get the point.

Fortunately, Jesus has a loophole for us here.

The first servant owes a *huge* debt. Huge. Like a whole country's worth of money. Like Beyonce's, Elon Musk's, or Jeff Bezos' money. The parable is based on the idea that wealthy people had property managers, who were supposed to extract money from small farmers, artisans, and fisher people, and funnel the money up to the landowner. One writer (Stanley Saunders) said that, "In the Mediterranean economy, the goal was to pass a steady, acceptable flow of wealth further up the pyramid, while retaining as much as one could get away with for oneself..." This is your stressed-out middle manager, or the assistant principal at the school. Lots of stress, very little power.

For the first person, we can imagine the weight off his shoulders when the king forgives his debt. His burden vanishes. It's like having your mortgage paid off, or your student loans forgiven, times a thousand. This changes his whole life.

* * *

But the first servant forgets quickly. He doesn't remember how awful he felt, and that he received a huge gift. When he runs into the second servant, he won't let that other person off the hook. All of his relief and gratitude and thanksgiving are gone. He repays the gift of forgiveness with...more rage.

What are we supposed to learn from that?

Forgive people no matter what?

Is that what Jesus was getting at?

In telling this story, Jesus gave us a forgiveness loophole.

* * *

He said that forgiveness is like running a marathon, getting a graduate degree, learning to cook gourmet food, or woodworking. It takes practice. We don't get it right the first time, or the second, or even the seventh. We have to work at it.

We have to do it over and over.

Peter wanted to know how much we have to practice. What's the right number? He suggested what he thought was a big number. Depressingly, Jesus said *nope, that's not enough.*

All of us can count up to seven times. But by the seventy-seventh time, or seventy times seven, we have forgotten the math. If we were trying to keep track, we have missed a few checks in our little notebook. It's become a habit — it's the way we live. It's like brushing our teeth or taking a shower, like eating salad or exercising. It's how we see the world.

Jesus is telling Peter, and us, to get out of the counting business.

Stop doing the math and concentrate on forgiving people.

* * *

When we work on this, don't start with the partner who stole your money, or your self-esteem. Don't start with the abuser in your life. Don't start with the callous boss, or the person who diminishes you every day. And some people are beyond our forgiveness skills in this lifetime, and we have to leave them to God.

Start with the neighbor whose yard sign you hate. Start with the person who lets their dog poop on your lawn. Start with the neighbor who leaves their trash can out all week. Start with the online commenters and silently wish them well. Work up to friends and family members. We can spend our first lessons in forgiveness on the people who take up two parking spaces…or bring 29 items to the express lane at the food store…or the people who eat the last piece of cake and put the container back — and work our way up.

* * *

Jesus is getting us out of the math business. When we try to measure forgiveness, we always start in the wrong place.

We think we're the givers, and we forget that we're the receivers.

All of us began the same place as the servant who owed the king 10,000 talents. We have received abundant grace from God. We have received a tremendous gift from God. Perhaps we've also been forgiven by friends, children, and partners. Maybe co-workers, or church people.

We don't forgive because we're good at it.

We forgive because we're connected to a God who forgives us. We forgive each other because people give us this gift, too.

* * *

Jesus did give us a forgiveness loophole here.

I bet you won't need it, though.

Jesus set us free from random rage, and from being upset by strangers and neighbors. Jesus let us detach from the people who make our blood boil, whether it's in traffic, or about politics, or online. He wants us to see that we are all part of the same system, where our lives and our health and our success are connected.

By the time we know how to forgive seventy-seven times, it's a habit.

By then, we know how to see other people as human — flawed — doing the best they can.

By then, we know how to give the benefit of the doubt.

What Jesus asked is impossible, and still, we can see how it calms our lives down, and shows us our connections.

What Jesus asked is impossible, until we see how much we have been given, and how slow we are to pass it on.

By the time we get to seventy times seven, we know the hugeness of God's gift to us, and the smallness of our own efforts. By then, we know how impossible it is, and also how compelling to live this way.

What Jesus asked is impossible. And it's also the deepest way into God's love as a way of life. Darn it.

In the name of Jesus our teacher, Amen.

Proper 20 (25)
Matthew 20:1-16

The Joys Of
Waiting In Line

What was waiting in line like where you grew up?

Did people stand in an orderly line, waiting patiently?

Was it more energetic, with people pushing and shoving to get to the front?

Was there no such thing as a line — everyone was on their own to get to the front?

I grew up in the Midwest, as some of you did, and we are very serious about fairness. We will politely wait in line forever, as long as it seems fair, and as long as there's some progress.

Given that, when I heard this parable, I always imagined the workers standing in an orderly line, waiting to be picked for a day's work. Then I went to Italy and took a bus somewhere. There was a line when we started, and as soon as the bus appeared, it was everyone for themselves, pushing and shoving and making their own line.

Maybe my imagination about this story was all wrong.

That image is a better way to picture these workers waiting so eagerly for a day's work. Not standing in line, but so desperate to work that everyone is crowding forward and shoving to be chosen. "Take me." "No, me, I'm a better worker."

And is it also like being picked for soccer or kickball teams in elementary school?

First, the strong workers are chosen, and then the next, until the last workers waiting are the slowest and the weakest, the ones who need the job most. The ones who are older, or have a limp, or don't look very sturdy. Many of us would be in that group. They have the embarrassment of not being chosen.

They're not good enough, not strong enough, and now they worry about making enough money that day.

* * *

These workers in the vineyard are hired by the day, so their lives are precarious. Each day they have to search for work again. No work, no food. Perhaps they have families waiting at home, feeling the pinch of hunger.

The first workers to be chosen are thrilled — a full day's work, at the going rate. What luck! They know they have a good deal.

For some reason, the later workers don't give up and go home, figuring everything is over for the day. They keep waiting, with no guarantees. And they get hired with no guarantees. No one tells them how much they'll get paid. The owner tells the workers that he'll pay them "whatever is right." They have to work all day on faith. Maybe they're still nervous as they work, wondering if it will all work out.

When it's time to get paid, there's a surprise. Those nervous, hopeful last workers who were hired last get a whole day's wage. What a gift. Then the next-to-last workers get a whole day's wage. More rejoicing! Everyone ends up with enough. The weaker, slower workers who come later get the same wage, without having to wear themselves out.

Everyone has enough.

* * *

You would think this would be reason for celebration in the whole village.

Except...

The first workers get mad and forget that they're getting exactly what they agreed to. They're getting what they were happy about a few hours ago.

I can't say that I really blame them.

We know what point Jesus is trying to make, and it still feels unfair. As the noted preacher Barbara Brown Taylor says, [This] "is a little like cod liver oil. You know Jesus is right, and you know it must be good for you, but that does not make it any easier to swallow." [from *The Seeds of Heaven*]

* * *

We all know that cod liver oil feeling.

We all know that life isn't fair.

It's one of the first things our parents teach us. We see it lived out in our lives every day. Hard-working people lose their jobs. Young people get sick. Talented people get rejected because of the color of their skin, or how they live in the world. The faithful suffer as much as people without faith. People are battered and beaten by people who love them. The legal system works better when you have money. Not every talented kid gets to go to college. We feel sad every day, as we see the lack of fairness in our world.

Even when we have enough food, enough money, enough work, we look around at other people and compare ourselves to people who have more. Even when we have plenty, we start to think there's not enough. You know the feeling. We have a perfectly fine car, until we look at the neighbor's car. Our college is perfect for us, until we hear that someone else is going to Morehouse or Harvard. Our grades, our home, our salary, our children, our partner are all perfect for us, until we look at someone else's. And then we think we need more.

* * *

Since this is a parable, we start to think about where God is in the story. If God is the generous landowner, then there's another layer of unfairness for us, as church people. As church folks, we do a lot for God. We're organized, we work hard for God, we give our gifts and tithes, and so we know that we're the first workers. God gets a lot of our time, energy, ideas and money. We're right here on a Sunday morning, aren't we, while the heathens are out to brunch?

We picture ourselves as the first workers in the story, the ones who do the most.

More and more, though, I see how I'm really like the last workers. I see how flawed my work for God is, and how little I do, compared to what I've been given. I see that I'm getting so much more than I deserve. When I add up my privileges, they're huge. Being white, educated, middle class, straight, and healthy all add lots of ease and safety to my life, and I didn't do anything to earn those things. Over and over, I come too late and too slowly to what God invites me to do.

* * *

Our Bible translation of this story says that the landowner said to the grumbling workers: "Are you envious because I am generous?" In the original Greek, the owner said: "Is your eye evil because I am good?"

Um, yes, that's it exactly.

God's generosity to us is always great.

To other people, not so much. Our eye is evil, and we're unhappy when we see good things happening to someone else. We see the unfairness of it all. This isn't what we expected at all! They don't deserve it.

But, do we? Does anyone?

In her beautiful book, *The Soul of Money*, Lynne Twist said that the problem is inside us. We think we're not wealthy enough, thin enough, confident enough, fit enough, or don't have enough social media followers. The list is endless. She said, "By the time we go to bed at night, our minds race with a litany of what we didn't get, or didn't get done, that day. We go to sleep burdened by those thoughts and wake up to the reverie of lack…"

There's not enough, we think.

We're falling behind.

We deserve more.

Instead, she says, we should think about sufficiency.

Sufficiency, for her, is not a quantity. It's not an amount. You can't find it in the bank. She says, "it isn't two steps up from poverty or one step short of abundance…. It's an experience…a declaration...knowing that there is enough, and that we are enough."

Sufficiency is grace.

It's not our credit score, or the number of cars in the driveway, or the number of social media likes, or the number of family members we can help, or the number of commas in our bank account. It's feeling grateful, whether it's for beans and rice, or the view from the mansion. It's the moment the workers are paid, when everyone is happy, until they ruin it for themselves.

* * *

In our world, more is always better, and money is a measure of our worth. Seeing that we have enough is a place of spiritual learning. Experiencing sufficiency is a big spiritual challenge. But God invites us all — you, me, and all of our fellow workers for God to exist in that place of enough. God invites us to rejoice when we have what we need. God invites us to celebrate when others have enough. God offers us an invitation to stop, and pause, and to know that there's enough for everyone, if we're willing to live by grace, and to take steps to even out the injustices of our world.

There's so much we can worry about these days.

So much is uncertain. So much is unfair.

In my own life, I hope to take God up on that invitation to see where there is already enough.

I hope to become better at seeing where I have enough, and even more than enough, and letting some go, so others have enough.

I hope you will, too.

We don't have to stand in line for it or earn it.

We live by grace, and God has enough for all of us. God invites us to live in a place of generosity. The world isn't fair, and we have more than we deserve. Let's stop comparing, and live in a place of generosity, not lack. We can receive with thanksgiving, and give without counting.

In the name of our generous God, Amen.

You're Not The Boss Of Me

Once upon a time, when I served a church in Detroit, I was driving to work and had to slow down for an accident. A couple blocks from the church, I could see some people standing on the corner, and two cars that had crashed into each other. Both looked wrecked, and I could see a young couple — maybe late teens or early twenties — standing on the sidewalk, holding a very small baby. No stroller, no car seat, no jackets on themselves or on the baby.

I pulled over a half a block away, and walked back over to the young couple to see if I could help with anything. As I talked to them for a little while, the police officer walked over. He had a beautiful air of having seen everything in his decades of service, and yet still caring about people. He had plenty of time and compassion for this one particular couple in front of him.

After a bit, he turned away from them toward me, smiled at me, and asked exactly the right question. "And you are?"

He meant: "Who are you?" and also "What are you doing here?"

Those were the questions that the religious authorities are asking Jesus.

* * *

When we find him in this story, Jesus has been busy.

He came into Jerusalem on what we call Palm Sunday. He went from the palm parade to the temple, tipped over the tables, upset the buyers and sellers, and then went out. Then he had the nerve to come back to the temple to teach.

The religious leaders asked him exactly the right question. "Who are you?" and "What are you doing here?"

"By what authority..." the religious leaders asked Jesus, and you can see their point. He was not a priest, not a Levite, a teacher of the law, and he didn't have any formal training as a rabbi. What was this carpenter bumpkin, no matter how famous he might be in his home area, doing here in this magnificent temple? Who was he to be teaching here? Where was his degree, his endorsement from someone important, or the evidence of his successful internship?

* * *

This question of authority runs through this story, and, really, all the way through Matthew's gospel. It runs through our lives, too.

When Jesus was first baptized, God announced that Jesus was the beloved Son, "with whom I am well pleased." Authority there comes from God. After his resurrection, Jesus ended his time by saying to his friends, "All authority in heaven and on earth has been given to me." His authority now comes from within.

Noted preacher Tom Long (in the *Westminster Commentary on Matthew*) said that this passage contrasts human authority with divine authority. Human authority is about power. It comes from guns, money, power, or influence, or it can be delegated by other powerful people. "Divine authority, on the other hand, has to do with truth, the truth of God, the truth about who God made us to be. In the short run, human authority can appear to overwhelm divine authority — even to crucify it — but, ultimately, God's truth prevails."

"By what authority..." the priests and religious leaders asked Jesus, and he answered their question with another question. The people trying to trick him were stumped, so he told a short story, a mini parable, to make his point. There were two sons — there are two kinds of people. He was saying some of them look great on the outside, and yet they don't have the truth within them. Others don't look all that great at first glance, and they end up having inner truth.

Jesus was telling these leaders, who believed they were doing the right thing, to know that God sees the inside. They might look righteous, and yet God has a different measuring stick. The people they looked down on have a path into God's heart. The people they considered sinners, unclean, unrighteous, are in front of them in line for God's favor.

Writing about this passage, Brian Stoffregen says that the secret of this passage was the word translated as "to change one's mind." He says that a better translation might be "changing what one cares about." The people who first say *no* to God change their minds. They change what they care about. They change more than their minds — it's their whole lives.

And those people who change their minds, change their lives, and change their hearts have as big a claim on God as anyone else. For people who go to church every week, this is a hard story to swallow. If you give faithfully, pray hard, and work to make the world better, shouldn't you have a shortcut to God? Nope. The people who come late to the party have as much claim on God as anyone else. It's another version of last week's parable.

And, still, it's hard to take.

* * *

It's hard to take until we realize that, depending on the day, any of us could fall into either category.

We say *yes* to God, and then don't get around to praying every day, or giving money away generously. We love God, and still it's hard to put down the TV remote and to get up to feed the hungry or visit the sick.

Other times, we tell God we're not going to do something, no way, no chance, not happening, and then God sneakily gets us to do it anyway.

I suspect God has done in your life what God has done in mine.

You know how this works.

You didn't really plan to tutor kids or raise your grand-kids. You started out to buy a nice car and then ended up giving your money to a relative who needed it. You don't plan to spend your vacation working for the Red Cross, or taking kids on a mission trip, or you spend your weekends painting for an elderly neighbor, and then all of a sudden you are. We can say no to God, but God has a way of persisting.

But what does God want us to do?

It's hard to figure out where to start, in a world of so much need. When we have no idea what to do next, author Chris Guillebeau says to do two things:

1. Make something. It could be toast, an art project, or woodworking. It could be a table, a scarf, a song, or a pile of leaves in the back yard.

2. Help someone. Make a small gesture that will benefit someone. Give a McDonald's gift card to someone asking for money on the corner. Carry a few with you so you're ready. Drop off dinner for a busy family. Rake your neighbor's leaves.

* * *

In Matthew's gospel, for Jesus, faith was about action.

Faith is about what we do.

It's more than belief, it's how we live our days.

Like the religious leaders, we spend our lives asking Jesus questions. "Who are you?" "What are you doing here?"

And when people ask us who we are and why we're here, why we're helping, why we're giving our money and our time, we can say that we followed Jesus here.

Jesus might answer us with a question, like he did the religious leaders.

"How much are you willing to follow?"

"Are you ready to have your life changed?"

We can say *yes* and not live up to it.

Or, we can say *no* and then go ahead and do our best. Either way, Jesus is going to wiggle into any opening we give him, until we change what we care about...change how we spend our time...change how we give our money...change how we see the world.

It's not that Jesus *has* authority — he *is* the authority.

Our work is to keep changing our minds, not once, but over and over, to care more and more about what he cares about. Our work is to put on the mind of Christ, as Paul said. Every time we manage to do it, we come closer and closer to the world of God.

We come closer and closer to the one who is the authority for us, and our lives.

In the name of Jesus, Amen.

A Bad, Bad Dream

Do you have a recurring stress dream; one that comes to you over and over?

Maybe it's about a test that you forgot about and didn't study for? Maybe it is a meeting at work where you don't know anything? Perhaps it is a child in trouble, and you can't figure out how to help? Not to suggest more stressful things for you to fret about at night…

When I was younger, I would often dream that I was waking up in the hallway of the school, in my pajamas, and everyone was staring at me. Now, the dream that reoccurs is always that I'm supposed to do a wedding, and I haven't prepared, and I'm lost in the church. I can't find the couple, my robe is lost, or they're all waiting, and I'm not there. Whew. I feel a little stressed just thinking about it.

This parable that Jesus told has a dream-like quality to it. He told this at a time of great pressure for him, and it had the feeling of a familiar stress dream. We find him in Jerusalem, during the last week of his life. He has ridden into town, heard the acclaim of the crowds, turned over the tables in the temple, and, for good measure, cursed a fig tree that was empty of fruit. He's been teaching in the temple, trying to get his wisdom out into the world before his inevitable death comes.

This parable is set in a vineyard, an image that appears often in the scriptures. In the Bible, vineyards symbolize peace and prosperity. It takes a long time to grow grapes that are good for anything, so a vineyard is a sign of stability. After the flood, Noah gets off the boat, and plants a vineyard as a sign of hope. A vineyard means that no one is at war, and no one is on the run. A fruitful vine is often used as a symbol for the nation of Israel. But this vineyard, in the parable, becomes a place of violence, instead of peace. The caretakers were managing the place for their own gain.

Jesus asked the people listening to him what would happen to the caretakers who had been so negligent, and the people answered that the caretakers would be no more. The answer to their shoddy work was another act of violence.

Interestingly, Jesus himself never said this. He was about to be the victim of violence in a few days, and still he didn't commend violence to anyone.

The easiest interpretation is that God is the vineyard owner, and the current religious leaders are in charge. In this case, the religious authorities are the caretakers for God's people. If we follow the parable in a straight line, then God is going to depose them, and get someone new to run the vineyard. With this interpretation, we get a little whiff of satisfaction here. Ha! So there! The religious leaders are mean to Jesus, so God will be mean to them. We can get a little too pleased with this neat interpretation.

A parable is never that delightfully simple, though. Sadly.

* * *

People who interpret dreams say that we are every figure in our own dreams. Each person in the dream symbolizes some part of ourselves. If we treat the parable that way, each one of us is each of the characters in the story, at different times.

In some chapters of life, we're the caretakers.

When have you been in charge of something precious? We've all been entrusted with the care of the earth, and with the money that we have — small or large — to use for good in the world. In some seasons of life, we care for elderly relatives, and for the children in our lives. We mentor younger colleagues and students. We shepherd different ministries in the church, leading for a time and then stepping back.

In these times, we ask ourselves if we are being faithful to God as the stewards. How are we doing with what God entrusts to us?

* * *

Other times, our role is to be the messengers from God, who keep coming and coming with their message, and get such a violent reception. To our shame, the wider church has often been hostile to messages from our LGBTQ+ siblings, and from people of color who remind us that we're not as progressive as we think we are. It's hard to hear messengers who talk about social justice and care for creation. It's even difficult to hear people who advocate for a new color of carpet, or a new hymnal.

In these times, we need God's strength to keep bringing a word from God, and all of us need to be wise and thoughtful listeners.

* * *

On other days, we are the vineyard owner, loving someone or something so deeply that we keep hoping for change. We send message after message that never gets heard. We keep trying, even when it doesn't make logical sense. We might be talking to a partner who has struggles with addiction or violence or trying to reach a boss with anger issues. We might be trying to reach a child who needs help, or a neighbor who shouldn't live alone anymore. We feel the pain of our messages going unheard. We pray for the energy to keep trying, and the wisdom to know when to stop and move on.

This parable has all kinds of echoes in our lives, as we find ourselves in different roles at different times.

Sharing the parable, Jesus made himself clear, telling the people listening that the realm of God will be taken away from them, and given "to a people that produces the fruits of the kingdom." Then his listeners recognized themselves in the story and were angry.

Where do we recognize ourselves?

The parable invites us to see where we are in this story. Our place can change, because God is never done with us.

* * *

In the way that dreams are timeless, all of this takes much longer than we imagine. The writer and artist Edward Hays says that in every big effort of our lives, we "must learn how to suffer the time of growth." He wrote that procrastination is a love affair with a mythical tomorrow where everything is better. Patience, however, "is full, pregnant with dreams, hopes, ideas, and with peace…Patience is loving and dynamic surrender."

In whatever role we are in, in this story, we need the gift of patience to live in it fully.

And in that patient faith, God makes us part of the divine story.

God is always dreaming about a world full of truth, justice and grace. God invites us to join in that holy dream of a world transformed, and of our lives renewed and made whole.

God summons us into this recurring dream, one that brings us no fear and abundant joy.

In the name of God the dreamer, and Jesus our teacher, Amen.

Let's Get This Party Going

One way to get people's attention is to have a coffin at your birthday party.

An entrepreneur in California, Michael Hebb, may have hosted the world's strangest birthday party when he did just that. He invited family and close friends to his party, and then pall bearers carried in a coffin, with Hebb inside. For three hours, he stayed in the coffin, silent and motionless, while people talked about what he meant to them. There were lots of tears, and lots of laughter, as Hebb got his wish — for people to talk openly about his death.

Most parties aren't that unusual — but this party that Jesus told about came close.

Jesus told this parable about what should be a fantastic banquet, but no one wanted to go. The king sent out his servants to invite people to his banquet. In that day, without texts, evites, phones, or calendars, the host sent the servants out ahead of time to tell people to be ready when the final invitation came. When the party was actually ready, the servants returned to tell people it was time to come. The guests were expected to get ready in the meanwhile — finish up other obligations and to be prepared. When the invitation in our story went out, it was the second invitation — people who had already been invited once. But, even the reminder wasn't enough to get people there.

* * *

In this parable, there are two kinds of judgment.

Some people refused the invitation and mistreated the king's messengers. Then there's the guest who came to the feast but refused to put on the proper garment. He accepted the invitation, and then failed to follow through on the last step. In that day, for a fancy wedding like that, the host supplied the robe. The guest only had to put it on — but, for some reason, he didn't.

That scene has always puzzled me. Why would the guest accept the invitation, go to all the trouble to get there, and then refuse to take the last step?

The traditional interpretation of this parable is that the king was a stand-in for God. In Jesus' time, the people who refused the invitation were the religious insiders. They wouldn't come when God invited them, and so God replaced them, turning to the hungry, the lowly, and the marginal, and inviting them in.

In our time, Lutheran pastor Brian Stoffregen suggested that the judgment here is for any of us who believe we have an inside track to God's party. The parable is, he wrote about our "smugness and laziness at being on the inside. We might say that God didn't want us to just wallow in divine grace. God expects more from us. Just getting to God's party isn't enough."

And the traditional view of this parable is that the final, unrobed guest lacked something for the realm of God. Some scholars believe that the missing garment represents righteousness. Others believe that it was repentance. Either way, God's invitation came, and he was not ready.

* * *

But Jesus never told a story with just one simple meaning.

He wanted his original listeners, and us, to keep turning this over in our minds, to come back to it as we work, drive, wash dishes, and mow the lawn. For fifty years or so after Jesus' death, people told stories about him, until they were written down into the gospels. We can see how this one would intrigue people, and they would keep telling it, and thinking about it. We can do the same.

For us, the parable is about how we live in God's presence now.

Are we hearing God's invitations? Being in the presence of God is like a banquet, but sometimes we miss the party and choose to sit home eating Door Dash instead.

If God called up and invited us to a party, of course we would know to say *yes* to that.

If God sent a text telling us to get out of our pajamas and get over here, we would accept. But the invitation isn't always that clear.

In my life, and maybe in yours, God's invitations come in disguise.

The invitation comes hidden as a task, or a challenge. It comes as an invitation to volunteer, or to serve on a committee, and we don't think we have anything to offer. Or the invitation comes in the form of a neighbor child who needs a friend, and we miss it because we don't want to meddle. The invitation comes to work at the food bank on a Saturday, and we miss it because we have soccer, or work to catch up on.

Like the people in the parable, God invites us to the banquet, and we miss the invitation. We're busy, or tired, or the invitation looks like something else.

* * *

Other times, we get there, and then we're the guest who won't put on the robe. We can't join all the way in.

All of us have places where we hold back from God. We're ready to give our time, and then we hold back on our money. Or perhaps we write generous checks, but choose to hold onto our worries, keeping them secret and silent. Maybe we pray deeply and often, and then forget to notice our neighbors. We do too much and miss God's offer to take a rest. We miss the next step of putting on the wedding garment and really joining God's party.

That guest without the wedding garment at the great feast? He gets there, but without any passion or joy in being invited. He doesn't care enough to be fully present. What if we're that guest? We accept the invitation, and all along, we're still looking for a better offer.

40

When God invites us, this is the better offer — the best we can do. This is the party of a lifetime, when we join in God's work.

* * *

The late Tony Campolo, in *Let Me Tell You a Story*, saw the world like no one else. He was a great storyteller, and he told a story about traveling to Haiti with an organization that developed schools for children there. Most of the children they served were so poor that their families gave them to other families who could feed them, and these children worked as servants for most of the day. School was scheduled from the late afternoon into the evening. The children were already tired from working all day, but he said, attended diligently because learning to read and write gave them more options out of their grinding routine.

One night, he said, he was returning to his hotel when three girls approached him. "Mister," the first one said, "for ten dollars you can have me all night long." He looked at her a little stunned, but realizing how desperately poor they were, and how far ten dollars would go. He looked at the second one. "For ten dollars, Can I have you all night long, too?" She nodded her approval. So did the third girl.

"Ok," he said. "I have thirty dollars. I'm in Room 210. Come in half an hour. All three of you."

He rushed up to his room, and called down to the front desk, telling the concierge that he wanted every Disney movie they had. Anything by Disney, please bring it to the room right away. He called down to the restaurant, asking for banana splits, as huge as possible, with extra whipped cream, extra nuts, and extra cherries. Send up four of them.

He and these young girls watched the movies, and ate the ice cream, and then the girls finally fell asleep about one in the morning. He watched them sleep, and thought, "Nothing's changed. Tomorrow night, they'll be back on the street. Nothing's changed."

Then, he said, the Spirit spoke to him, and said "But for this one night, you let them be little girls again. Tonight, they got to be kids." That little party, he says, in Room 210 of the Holiday Inn, was a gift from the Holy Spirit.

* * *

And so is every invitation to God's party.

We're the invited guests, beloved by God. We're invited into a life of joy and abundance, even when the world around us is harsh.

And we are also the servants, called to go out and bring people to the party — to invite them to the feast God has for all of us. The story says that the good and the bad are invited together. We don't sort out the guests, and it's not our job to judge, and say who's worthy or not. Our work is to celebrate, and to invite, and to put on the garment of a full life with God.

God's divine feast includes us all and awaits us all.

The banquet is ready.

Let us join in the joy of God's presence, in every way we can. In the name of Jesus our host, Amen.

Does Jesus Use Cryptocurrency?

Does it ever concern you that you might be turning into your parents?

Or maybe your favorite aunt or uncle, or a beloved grandparent?

You admonish a child, and you hear your dad's voice come out. You rinse out a plastic bag so you can use it again, and find your mother living inside you? Maybe it's making a certain food a certain way, or using a phrase you vowed never to use on your own kids. My own mother was famous in the family for saving perfectly good wrapping paper that had only been used once…well, or maybe twice…or even a few Christmases. It still makes my fingers twitch a little to throw wrapping paper away. Every year, I feel compelled to save a nice big piece to use again next year.

The people we spend time with leave a peculiar imprint on us.

Bosses who take time with us, choir leaders, and scout leaders. The neighbor we visit every week after school. The aunt or uncle who teaches us their skills. The teacher who sees the world a certain way.

The imprint is a connection, a kind of belonging to each other.

* * *

When we see the imprint on a coin, there's a similar recognition.

In Jesus' time, the first thing new emperors did was to have coins made, with their image on them. Just like, in our day, new governors change the road signs to say "Welcome to the state of XXX, Governor XXX."

The coins with the image of the Roman emperor paid one of the taxes levied on the Jewish people. We know of at least four taxes that the Jewish people paid.

This one — that people are asking Jesus about -is *"kensos,"* borrowed from the Latin word census. This was an annual tax, paid to Rome, for everyone old enough to work. It was about a day's wages, paid once a year.

Every time someone paid this tax, it was a bitter reminder that a foreign power was profiting from their labor and their homeland. Only Roman coins could be used to pay the tax. The coins proclaimed that emperor was divine — a graven image that went against their faith.

This would be like if each one of us paid an annual tax to China, in Chinese coins, to service the US debt that China holds. It would be tough to swallow as citizens, even without the religious layer.

So, when we hear this question, we can feel the trap for Jesus.

The questions seem simple, and yet the people asking couldn't be more different. We have the Pharisees, the religious rulers, and the Herodians, a party loyal to Herod, whom the Jewish people hated. This is like lining up Travis Kelce and Yo-Yo Ma, or President Trump and Representative Occasio-Cortez. You see them together and start to wonder what's going on.

When Jesus asked one of the crowd for a coin, he was setting his own trap. When the religious leaders handed one over, they showed that they were carrying around a graven image. They were breaking the Jewish law by doing that.

* * *

Give to the world what belongs to the world, Jesus says. That's easy enough.

In fact, we can't escape it. We have taxes taken out of our wages. We get bills for the heat, for the lights, for our credit cards. There's no eluding sales tax when we buy something. We need money to buy food and clothes and gas for the car.

But God doesn't send a bill.

How do we give to God what belongs to God?

* * *

We can try to divide up our lives, between our weekday selves and our Sunday selves. Work some days, spiritual life other days. We give God our tithe, and then we can use all the rest, right? Until we realize what Jesus is saying…that everything belongs to God. The business opportunity that made our bottom line? Gift from God. The bonus at work? Gift from God. The inheritance from a loved one? Gift from God. The raise at work? Gift from God.

* * *

Lynne Twist, in her lovely book, *The Soul of Money*, tells about the time her mother was near the end of her life. She was in hospice care, and she wanted to be sure she was leaving people with what she wanted them to have.

She got out a piece of paper and made a list of the people whom she had known over the years. She asked her daughter to make some calls for her, and she started at the top of the list. First, was her dry cleaner. When they answered, she asked for Ken, the manager. She said something like, "Ken, this is Mrs. Tenney. I'm dying, and I'm talking to my daughter about the people who have made my life so special. You and your staff have helped me by making sure I had clean, fresh clothes. I appreciate everything you've done for me."

She made these calls to many places—her favorite restaurant, talking to the chef, her car repair place, the person behind the make-up counter at the department store, the people who cut her hair, and so on. She thanked each person, and told them that when the time came, she would like them to come to her funeral and sit behind her family.

After each call, her daughter wrote down the name and phone number.

Mrs. Tenney had paid for these services, and yet she found a layer of connection in each transaction. She wanted people to know that more had happened than just a simple exchange of goods and services. People had left an imprint on her life.

Next were her grandchildren.

She wrote a letter to each one and sent them money before her death. She asked each one of them to tell her what they planned to do with the money, so she could share in the fun of their plans. It wasn't a big amount. What she wanted to emphasize was the relationship.

Then she paid all of her bills and paid for her funeral. At the end of her life, she was almost out of money, which made her proud. She thought about the gifts she had made to organizations over the years, and the people the money had helped. By the end of her life, she felt like she had used everything God had entrusted to her.

* * *

We need apps, Venmo, and credit cards to interact with the world, but every time we do, we are also interacting with God. Every time we spend money, or save it, or give it away, we're reflecting the God who gives us so much. We're reflecting the image of God within us, as we use money.

Jesus is nearing the end of his life here, and he wants us to know what he knows: it all belongs to God. We all belong to God.

We are meant to return our whole selves to God — in our giving, in our saving and in our spending.

God doesn't have coins, or paper money. The thing stamped with God's image is us. We carry God's imprint with us, in everything we do…everything we spend…everything we give.

We are God's traveling coins, carrying God's image through the world.

We give to God what belongs to God, and it turns out that what belongs to God is…everything.

You, and me, and even Caesar.

In the name of a generous God, Amen.

So Many
Blooming Questions

If you spend any time with young children, you know they ask a lot of questions. They haven't been trained not to ask them, so the questions come thick and fast, as fast as they pop into their heads.

"Why is grandpa's skin wrinkled?"

"Why do we have to eat green beans?"

"Where do babies come from?"

Some are embarrassing, pointing out different body types and skin colors.

Teenagers have other questions.

"Does this outfit look okay?"

"How can you tell if someone likes you?"

"What should I do when I feel unsafe?"

"Am I going to get into college somewhere?"

I love it when guests and new people come to the church because they see things that I miss. "Why do you do it that way?" "Why don't you have this program or that ministry?"

Our scriptures the last few weeks have taken us on a tour of the questions people ask Jesus. This is the last in a long series, and Jesus has the last word. He asks the last question, and then there are no more.

* * *

For Jesus, every group in town had come to him with a question, hoping to trip him up. They sent a lawyer, an expert in the Jewish law, to ask Jesus which commandment was the most important. There were 613 commandments in the law, so this was an impossible question. Any ordinary person would have been stumped — is it the rule about the Sabbath, or the one about giving a tithe? Is it an obligation to the poor, or to the temple? It's impossible to pick.

Jesus saw the real question behind this question.

His answer evoked the great Jewish prayer, the Shema, taken from Deuteronomy. "Love the Lord your God with all your heart and with all your soul and with all your strength. Deuteronomy (6:5) He added to it a word from Leviticus (19:9-17) reminding the people of the ancient obligation to their neighbors.

As writer John Petty said, "Jesus also did something no one today would dare try: He changed this ancient statement of faith. He changed *dunameos* (strength, power) to *dianoia* (mind, thought) — not love God with all one's strength, as Deuteronomy has it, but love God with all one's mind." (from his blog)

Jesus was adding a layer to the life of faith. The principle underneath everything God does — Love. The inspiration for the prophets? Love. What leads us into conversation with God? Love. What should motivate all of our acts of service? Love.

Jesus changed the question — it's not rules, it's about how we live.

* * *

Jesus also managed to cover all ten commandments in two sentences. Love God — that covers the false gods and graven images, honoring the Sabbath, and taking the Lord's name in vain. Love your neighbor — that covers all the coveting, honoring one's parents, stealing, murder and adultery. Very simple. So simple that it's tempting to remind us all to go out and do it and then sit down.

That's the whole sermon, isn't it? Do we need to say anything more?

Before you look at your watch and get excited, there is one more thing.

* * *

The intriguing thing is the second part, where Jesus asked the question. In all the times I've read this passage, I've mentally skipped over this second part, thinking it wasn't all that important. It's confusing and doesn't seem to add anything.

Turning the tables, Jesus asked, "What do you think of the messiah? Whose Son is he?" This question was not about genealogy, but about God's plans for the messiah. His question was: will the coming messiah be a king like David, in the pattern of David? Of course, everyone answered. This was the assumption of the time, that the messiah would be a conquering king. Everyone was hoping for relief from Rome's oppression. Jesus quoted a psalm to make his point, and he's saying that the messiah doesn't fit any mold people can devise. Look for something different.

Look for a messiah who's going to remake the world.

Look for a messiah whose law is love.

Look for the people who know how to follow.

* * *

If that's the case, I'm a little afraid of the questions Jesus might ask me.

When he looks at my ability to love God with all my heart and spirit, and my attention to my neighbor, he might ask me things like:

Why don't you pay attention to who makes your clothes, and whether they're made in sweatshops?

Every time you eat a strawberry, why don't you pause and think about the person who picked it?

Why aren't you more patient, and more generous with your judgments?

Why so much attention to the neighbors you know, and so little to the ones you don't? How can you drive past people begging on the street and not stop?

No doubt Jesus has questions for all of us. No doubt he has questions for us all, as a church. Churches often ask ourselves what we're known for. What stands out about us?

What would our neighbors say? Oh, they're the church that
_____.

The nightmare answer is that people say, "Oh, there's a church there? I had no idea." Or, that's the church where the people are mean. Or, I went there once, and someone told me I was in their seat. Not that that could ever happen here.

Jesus invites us to ponder the answer to: Our church is best known for _____?

What would it be?

And what questions do we have to ask ourselves to get there?

* * *

Going even farther down this road, following the one who asked so many questions, we have our own questions to ask, too.

In our own lives, are we filled with the love and grace of God?

As a faith community, are we guided by loving God and our neighbors?

As citizens of this country, are we using our votes and our voices to bring God's love to illuminate our choices?

Jesus managed to simplify all the law and the prophets into this two sentences. He covered all 613 laws, and made the foundation easy to understand. Along the way, he made it all a lot harder to do.

It's easy to follow rules, and hard to change our hearts.

It's easy to check off items on a list, and hard to shape our days around love. We all fail regularly, all the time, and still, Jesus keeps asking the question, and so we keep trying to answer with our whole hearts, hoping to do better and better each time.

In the name of the unexpected messiah, Amen.

The Unchanging Truth...
That Changes

Now that my parents are gone, I've been reflecting on the vital principles I was raised on. These things were presented to me as the sacred truth.

Hard ice cream is better than soft.

Vegetables should be boiled within an inch of their lives.

Ann Arbor is the center of the known universe.

The Rose Bowl exists for Michigan to play in it.

The book is always better than the movie.

Thanksgiving dinner should be served at 2:00 pm, accompanied by lots of pie. I'm still slightly shocked that I married into a family that serves Thanksgiving dinner at 4:00, and dessert is cake. No, no, no — it just can't be.

* * *

If we grew up in a church, we were raised with other certainties.

The Pharisees were narrow-minded people, always opposed to Jesus. They were legalistic — judgy — rule-bound. If the Bible was a movie playing in our heads, they would have worn the black hats.

We've been trained for years to know that were enemies with Jesus.

To set the stage, our Bible mentions three different Jewish groups.

We have Pharisees, who were laypeople and scribes. Say, these are like the Methodists and Presbyterians. They love order and have rules for their faith. The Essenes were more radical, living in a community apart, and the source of the Dead Sea Scrolls. Say, they're like the Mennonites. The Sadducees were the priests and wealthy people. The Episcopalians of Jesus' day. They were the most conservative, holding strongly to the written word of God, revealed in the Hebrew scriptures. Typically, the Pharisees and the Sadducees were in conflict with each other.

The Pharisees were educated people, admired for their righteousness. They were examples of faithful living. They were influential people, trying to preserve the Jewish faith in a nation overrrun with foreign people and beliefs. They took tradition and the Torah seriously, and made them apply to daily life. They brought faith home, and taught people that gathering around the dinner table is also a place to find God. As it is when you wash your hands and when you prepare food. This is enviable, to find God in all the routines of daily life.

* * *

So why did Matthew portray them so negatively?

If we dig deeper, was Matthew actually being a jerk here?

Matthew wrote the most Jewish of the four gospels.

He wrote his gospel for Jewish people who had come to believe in Jesus. He fitted Jesus carefully into the narrative of Jewish history.

For the Pharisees, these new followers of Jesus were upstarts with no principles.

For the followers of Jesus, the Pharisees were judgy nitpickers.

When Matthew wrote down his gospel, in about the year 80 CE, a break-up was coming, or had happened.

Bible scholars say that Matthew's fixation on the Pharisees suggested that his community was in a place where they had considerable influence. (Julie Galambush, *The Reluctant Parting*) The synagogues were starting to turn against the followers of Jesus. The Pharisees and Jesus' followers were dividing into different groups, with different worship locations and practices. Before this, everyone was a Jew, some who followed Jesus and other who did not, yet still all Jews.

It was possible that Matthew's audience was once part of a synagogue, and had been expelled. They definitely knew they were unwelcome. If you've ever left a church, or been part of a church fight, you know how painful this is. The wounds last a long time.

So, Matthew set out to show how the Pharisees were wrong. More than any other gospel, he made the Pharisees into archenemies of Jesus.

"Unless your righteousness exceeds that of the scribes and Pharisees," said Jesus, "you will never enter the kingdom of heaven" (5:20). This could have been a compliment...and given Matthew's preoccupation with the Pharisees, maybe it was not. This was a low bar, Matthew was saying.

* * *

The bigger problem is how the Christian church has used these texts and others as a basis for looking down on our Jewish neighbors. Over the years, the wider church has taken these texts as a license to hate Jewish people. We — the wider church — have something called "replacement theology," where Jewish people, by killing Jesus, forfeited all of God's promises. In this view, all of God's blessings now belong to people who followed Jesus, and no longer to the Jewish people.

The weird irony is that the Christian church has become the Pharisees.

To anyone walking by a church while walking their dog, taking a run, going to work, or looking for a place to sleep, we look judgy. Rule-bound. Exclusive. Old-fashioned. Mean-spirited.

Of course, we know that we're not, and yet we live in a world where people throw up their hands and give up on church. The biggest denomination in the country right now is the "nones," people who don't find any church hospitable.

Still, we know people are still deeply spiritual: they live it out with yoga, community service, Tarot cards, retreats, astrology, meditation, and being in nature.

* * *

The Pharisees remind us that certainty is great for religion. But any true connection with God is about mystery. We, just like Matthew, just like the Pharisees, just like the church for 2,000 years, keep seeking the perfect balance of both.

Over and over in history, people of faith have had an experience of God, get organized, and then the next step becomes having rules, which means some people don't belong. So those people break away, and start something new, and that eventually needs rules. Someone always wants to make rules, and someone always comes along to poke at the rules and remind people of the Spirit.

Religion needs both the container and the contents. The container is the denomination, the building, the bylaws, the classes, the cookies. The contents are the way we meet God. We need both. We live in a tender balance between the two.

The Pharisees and Jesus all wanted the same thing — more of the presence of God in everyday life. They both remind us to want that, too.

As they both teach us, may we find God in all that we do. Amen.

All Saints Day
Matthew 5:1-12

God's Weird Mystery Gifts

Human beings are wired for connection, scientists tell us.

To maintain those connections, we're always scanning each other for clues.

As social beings, we want to know what's going on with our fellow humans.

With people we know well, we look to see if they're in a good mood or having a rough day. We try to read our kids, grandkids, and young friends to see what their interests are. We're always watching the boss for signs of pleasure or upset.

When we meet a stranger, we look at their clothes, bumper stickers and social media to see what they believe. Liberal or conservative? Friendly or grumpy? Fitting in with the world, or working to be different?

In this passage, the people listening to Jesus speak were wondering who he was. And he was there to explain. It was early in his work, and Jesus has just called his followers. These were his very first words as a public preacher.

* * *

We call this passage "The Beatitudes," taken from the Latin word "blessed."

This is one of those parts of the Bible that is almost too familiar to churchgoers. If it's new to you, then you have an advantage. When we know these words well, they lose their impact for us. Hearing them fresh is a gift.

When we really pay attention, they're not so charming.

As one author says, "Whenever we hear the Beatitudes, we are struck with their poetic beauty and, at the same time, overwhelmed by their impracticality for the world in which we live. We admire the instruction, but we fear the implications of putting the words into actual practice. [Charles James Cook, from *Feasting on the Word*, Year A, Volume 1]

These are nice words — for other people.

For ourselves, they're too impractical...too lofty...not workable in our lives...accessible only to true saints, whom we're content to admire, but not ready to emulate.

* * *

Of all the gospels, Matthew was the most interested in Jesus as a teacher. Matthew remembers fewer miracle stories than Luke and Mark, and more teaching. For Matthew, Jesus announces who he is with a sermon on a mountain. As soon as we hear about the mountain, we're meant to think of Moses, and understand Jesus as the heir of Moses, taking up God's work in the spirit of Moses. This is a new set of commandments.

The Beatitudes would have had a familiar sound in Jesus' day. Preachers often used this same beginning "Happy are those who" ...or "Blessed are they who..." Some of the psalms contain the same language.

Scholars are divided about the Beatitudes.

Some firmly believe that they're part of the wisdom tradition of the Bible, giving people words for daily living. They talk about life in the beloved community, and how God's promises are fulfilled right here and right now. These are all words about how we live together.

Other scholars firmly believe that they're a message about the coming kingdom of God. Jesus was a prophet of God's kingdom — he was announcing the dramatic beginning of God's world on earth. This was about the fulfillment of God's promises — even more than commandments, but a description of how God's world works.

In other places, Jesus said: "You have heard it said...but I say to you.... ." Each one of these phrases could easily start with that. We can hear it, unsaid, behind the words. "You have heard it said that wealth is a sign of God's favor, but I say to you: Blessed are those who are poor and hungry." "You have heard it said, Blessed are the successful, but I say to you, blessed are the hungry." As he kept talking here, Jesus was making it clear that the kingdom of heaven belongs to the lost, the sorrowful, and the humble.

But, really, who would want these blessings? "Blessed are the poor in spirit...blessed are those who mourn...blessed are the meek." These first three are about a sense of emptiness in our lives. Blessed are the people with an ache in the soul. And the people who grieve. And the meek. In our can-do American culture, that one is especially alien. How will we ever get anywhere if we're meek?

These words are alien to a particular kind of Christian faith, where people are told that if they have enough faith, God will show up with a new car, plenty of money, and a life with no sorrow. When that doesn't happen, people feel like it's their fault, for not having enough faith. Jesus says something different. God is not a magician, doling out goodies. Instead, God is the presence beside us in our sorrow.

* * *

As we remember beloved people today, on All Saints Sunday, we recall the places where they embodied these blessings. We remember their gifts in serving the church, and in touching our lives. And, for true memories, we also have to remember their faults. We think about the places they struggled to be God's people, and the ways they grew over the years.

As we walk in their footsteps, we know that all of these odd blessings give us places for God to work on us.

The first few Beatitudes give us the emptiness that allows God's spirit to come in. As successful people, we think that we create our own success. We worked hard for what we have in life, we studied hard, we used all the discipline we have to get where we are. There's a lot to be said for that. But if we never feel a sense of emptiness, there's no room for God's presence. Our poverty of spirit makes room for God's abundance.

Once we know that emptiness, we can move on to the next three Beatitudes, which are about attitudes of the spirit. "Blessed are those who hunger and thirst for righteousness. Blessed are the merciful. Blessed are the pure in heart."

These, um, blessings don't seem like that much fun either. Hunger and thirst for righteousness means that we see the world all too clearly, and we hunger for more. We see the injustice of the world, the violence between people, a world that allows children to be hungry, and we live with heavy hearts. We see hatred for the LGBTQ+ community disguised as religion, and our spirits are weighed down. That's a gift? To see pain and suffering everywhere we go?

Sadly, by now it's too late for us.

Once we learn to love being poor in spirit, once we learn to mourn as a way of life, once we learn to treasure our meekness as well as our strength, then the rest follows right behind. It's too late for us to back away from God's strange gifts. We understand that we are blessed when we don't fit with the things the world finds important. Blessed are we when we have taste for faithful living and justice. A gift for looking at people with compassion instead of judgment. A clarity about the world and its shiny pleasures that allows us to see past them to see God.

The final three are about how we act in the world. Now we move from inner work to outer action. "Blessed are the peacemakers. Blessed are those who are persecuted. Blessed are the people who are despised and lied about, for the sake of God."

These blessings are painful gifts, too, but now we're on the hook. Blessed are those who love peace more than being right, for they belong to God in a special way. Blessed are the people who don't care what other people think, who can chart their own course in life.

By now, we've been following God down this road, and we don't know how to do anything other than to be peacemakers, or stand up for what we believe, because we've been accepting these strange gifts from God all the way along in our journey of faith. First, we receive these blessings in who we are as people of faith, and then in how we see the world, and finally in how we live in it. Little by little, God is making us into people of mercy and peace and clear purpose.

Once we start, these are gifts we can't return or exchange. We change to fit these mystery gifts from God.

* * *

So, are the Beatitudes about something we're supposed to do, or about who we are? Are they about our life in the present, or about the future when God comes to rule on earth?

Yes.

They're about a peculiar way of seeing the world — seeing it as God sees it. Seeing the value in poverty and emptiness of spirit, in our grief and our longing for more. Seeing the world with meekness and a gift for making peace. God's grace comes to us in our longings, our losses, our places of need.

We have our own Beatitudes, too.

Blessed are the odd gifts of our own lives, for they reveal the holy in new ways.

Blessed are the gifts of a difficult child, or a long illness, for these times open the door to seeing God in new ways. Blessed is the pain of unemployment, for the way it grows out trust. Blessed are the times of church struggle, for they teach us to develop our wisdom, and our boundaries. Blessed are the seasons of personal doubt, for they teach us to ask better questions. Blessed is the ache of grief, for it reminds us of the gift of love.

And blessed are we who have remembered our loved ones today.

Blessed is this community of faith, for we are richer for the gifts of the saints we remember today.

Blessed is the God who lives in our places of emptiness, and blessed are we who find God in the open spaces, and in the hurts of our lives.

In the name of the one who gives us these mysterious gifts, and who walks with us in every time of life, Amen.

The People Who Forgot To Set Their Alarms

This parable is, frankly, annoying.

We find Jesus at the end of his life, sharing all the wisdom he can before his death, and yet this parable doesn't fit with the rest of the message of Jesus.

Why can't the attendants who have enough oil share with the others?

Is Jesus applauding them for being selfish?

And why should they be blamed when the bridegroom is late? Isn't he at fault here, if we need to blame someone?

* * *

The setting of this parable would have been familiar to anyone who listened. If someone told you something happened at a wedding, you could picture the typical wedding for your friends or family.

In Jesus' day, weddings were huge celebrations, and there was no save-the-date card. The couple was legally joined when they were betrothed to each other, a much stronger bond than our modern engagements. Some years would go by, and when the groom was ready to support the bride, she moved from her father's home to his home.

The groom and his relatives and friends would come to the bride's home, where she waited with her relatives and friends. Then he would take her back to his home, and the celebration would happen there. That wedding celebration is the setting of this parable. Everyone is waiting for the party, for the big celebration.

There's was no texting to say, "On the way, be there soon." No way to call ahead and say when they would arrive. Time was much less precise then, so we can understand why the bridesmaids fall asleep waiting.

* * *

So, what's the difference between the so-called wise bridesmaids and the so-called foolish bridesmaids? Interestingly, they all fall asleep. There's no difference between how they wait. They are all family members or close friends of the bride. They all want to see a happy celebration.

In Jesus' hands, this story of waiting for the bridegroom becomes an image of waiting for the reign of God — waiting for the big celebration, when God's grace and love rule the world.

As always, when we read the gospels, we think about two layers of time. What was happening when Jesus said these things? And what was happening when the writers wrote everything down, thirty, forty, or fifty years after Jesus died? In the arc of the gospel stories, we're nearing the end of Jesus' life, and he's preparing his followers to live without him. He's talking about what they need to do to prepare.

A few decades later, when the gospels were written down, this same message had extra urgency. The early believers expected Jesus back at any moment, and the waiting felt long, and hard. The huge Jerusalem temple had been destroyed — surely that was a sign of the end. It would be as if the White House, the Pentagon, and Silicon Valley were all leveled, and we were waiting to see what was next.

So, what should they do with the delay?

How should they wait?

Matthew was trying to answer that question with this parable.

For Matthew, the people of God had one job — to proclaim the presence of God in the world. They were waiting eagerly for the return of Jesus, and they wanted to be ready.

Matthew used light in a particular way. For him, light was a symbol of how we live in the world, the good that we do. The lamps were the key to the parable. In another place, Jesus said, "Let your light shine before men and women that they may see your good works and give glory to your father in heaven." And also, "The righteous will shine like the sun in the kingdom of their Father."

Get out there and get those lamps lit, was the message.

This isn't about the oil — it's about how we spend our lives, so we're prepared to welcome the kingdom of God. How we spend our light. How we live in the world. We are being told not to let our lamps go out.

No matter how bleak things get…

No matter how slow…

No matter how dark…

keep your lamps lit.

* * *

Since a parable is like a dream, things don't line up precisely. For Jesus, it goes without saying that in ordinary life, people would share their oil, or their food, or their shelter with other family members who needed something. In everyday life, that was expected.

But the parable is about preparing for the realm of God.

Everyone has their own light to tend, their own work to do.

* * *

The same is true for us, in our layers of waiting. Each one of us has a lamp to keep burning.

For some, it's to keep quiet and learn, and for others it's simply to be safe in the world. For some it's to teach, to the extent of your energy, about what it's like to be of color, or to have a disability, or to be part of the LGBTQ community,or the experience of being an immigrant here.

For some, it is activism, and for others, it's learning to rest. For some, it's fiery work, and for others it's quiet.

We're waiting for things in our own lives — graduations, retirement, and new babies. We're waiting for operations, and new homes for new chapters of life. As a church, we're waiting and listening for God's direction. As people of faith, we're always waiting for the realm of God to break so fully into our world that we can't miss it. While we wait, we have the hard work of keeping our lights burning, even when the days are discouraging. We keep tending the flame of love, even when the world is full of shadows. We keep feeding the flame of compassion, even when the world wants to blow it out.

There is a job for each of us, until we live in the world God wants us to have.

* * *

The bridegroom — a stand-in for Jesus himself — is allowed to be late because God is not bound by our schedules and plans.

We are allowed to be annoyed, or disappointed, or glad. And still we have plenty to do while we wait.

We have lamps to light until God's presence is alive and full and complete among us. We have lamps to light, until we banish the shadows of everything that works against God.

We have lamps to light, until our world matches God's celebration.

In the name of the one who comes, and is coming, Amen.

Proper 28 (33)
Matthew 25:14-30

Gaining Weight For God

If I begin to tell you something with the words, "A man walked into a bar…" you settle back. You know a joke is coming. If you hear, "Once upon a time…" you know that's the start of a story.

The same thing happens here, as people are listening to Jesus.

Anyone listening to Jesus would have known right away that he was exaggerating to make his point. This is not a literal story. A man went on a journey, and entrusted his servant with five talents — a talent is 6,000 denarii. A denarius is the average daily wage, so this is a lifetime's worth of wages. It would be as if I started with "A boss entrusted her employee with a million dollars…" We would perk right up to hear that unusual tale.

In our world, it would be as if the boss is going out of town and she decided to dole out some assignments.

The first person is a great candidate for more responsibility: Ivy League education, graduate degree, well-liked, and he fit in with everyone at work. His parents were able to pay for college for him, so he didn't have any student loan debt. He can dress well and take people to lunch. He lived in a nice neighborhood where he felt safe, so he got to work well-rested, energetic, and full of ideas. He and the boss' husband were in the same fraternity, so they got together outside of work.

He got a plum assignment from the boss.

The second person was a good candidate for more responsibility. He had a college degree. His parents weren't so wealthy, so he was going to grad school at night. He didn't always seem like a go-getter because he was tired from going to school, but he was doing fine.

He got a nice assignment from the boss.

Oh, yeah, and the third person. The boss thought, *I guess I should give them something, too, even though they don't fit in with the rest of us. She's still working on her college degree, and she keeps making me sign forms to get the company tuition match. Annoying. As a single parent, she calls out of work when the child is sick, so she's not very dependable.*

She got an assignment that no one really cared about, with very scanty instructions about how to do it.

* * *

The story said that the landowner gave each person the money to match their ability...and the word "ability" can also be translated as power. The most powerful person got the most, which added even more to their power. The next person still got a substantial amount, and the least powerful person got the least. The first two made more money — but not by earning it.

When Jesus told this story, ancient Palestine had a lot of small farmers and fisherpeople, and a few very, very wealthy people. People of means used its wealth to make loans to peasant farmers so they could plant their crops. Interest rates were high, and the small farmers needed the money, so they used their farmland as collateral. After a bad year of farming, they ended up with debts they wouldn't pay. Eventually, they felt they might lose their farmland altogether. In this way, small, independent landowners turned into day laborers dependent on the owner for work. The household employees in our story were the ones who brokered these deals.

In Jesus' culture, it was shameful to have so much more money than the people around you. If you had that much, people believed, you should be sharing it. Over and over, when Jesus complained about the rich, it was because they were not using their money to help the people around them. People who study the ethics of Jesus' time say: "an increase in the share of one person automatically meant a loss for someone else. Honorable people, therefore, did not try to get more, and those who did were automatically considered thieves. Noblemen avoided such accusations of getting rich at the expense of others by having their affairs handled by slaves." (Malina and Rohrbaugh)

* * *

In our world, we're trained to think that bigger is better.

We turn right away to the first servant as a model.

But Jesus typically builds his parables from the bottom up. From the woman who lost a coin to the shepherd who lost a sheep to the father who lost a son. From the guests who wouldn't come to a banquet to the guests who would.

Storyteller Jesus had a surprise ending.

The third servant was the one to watch.

The third servant knew the landowner, and knew how the money was made. He knew that making money would do harm to someone else. The third servant had likely been yelled at by the landowner before, and likely would be again.

And so, this person opted out of the land owner's challenge. They were not playing this cruel game. They saw beyond the rules of the game to a place of compassion, even resistance to this unjust system.

* * *

We know this person, in our world.

This is the person who opts out of competition, and focuses on collaboration. This is the person who teaches us how to rest, instead of doing more and more and more until we're exhausted. This is the person who works to make the world better. This is the volunteer, the teacher, the first responder, the health care worker.

This is the single parent who gets to every single parent-teacher conference. This is the caregiver, sacrificing sleep. This is the person who knows how to say *no*. This is the dad with a second job so their child can play a sport. This is the person in your office who is worn out by explaining to everyone how people of color see things, or how Asian people view things. This is the weight some of you carry, accommodating to American culture all the time. This is your young friend who has been so judged and shamed by the church that they've given up on us, but not on doing good in the world.

We know this person.

By grace, we might be this person.

* * *

We've been trained to think, over the years, that the landowner is a stand-in for Jesus. That makes less and less sense to me. Jesus never praised people for participating in a cruel system; never lauded people for making a lot of money. Jesus was more interested in people giving money away than making it.

If anyone stood in for Jesus, it's the third servant. The one who doesn't play the game. The one who resists expectations. The who was cast into the outer darkness...and rises to live again, and to re-shape the world. That's a story we know.

* * *

In all the years I've heard this parable, I've heard the talent described as an ancient coin.

But I read recently that a talent is a measure of weight — the value of the talent depends on the metal. It can be gold, silver, bronze — the weight is the same. It's like a pound — a pound of feathers and a pound of lead weigh the same, but they're very different experiences. And like a pound of something, the value depends on the substance — a pound of gold is worth more than a pound of bread. Unless you're starving.

In the life of faith, we all weigh the same to start — we all have the same measure of love and forgiveness from God. But in the life of the world, some of us start with more than others. Some of us build on that and think we did well. Some of us start with very little and know that our worth in God. Some of us can see clearly where to give our weight away to anyone in need and so gain more.

* * *

The third servant is the one to watch. The one who knew that growing toward God was about the weight of our goodness, not our money. The weight of our compassion. The weight of our ability to say yes and no to the right things.

Our job is to grow, to gain weight — in the presence of God. To increase the places where God is alive in us, and in the world around us. To feel the weight of God's spirit in our lives, and to make it grow.

This is the story we want to be part of.

In Jesus' name, Amen.

Reign of Christ – Proper 29 (34)
Matthew 25:31-26

Everyone Is Clueless

"If it seems like it's too good to be true, it is."

Did your parents and aunts and uncles tell you that growing up? Or, some version of it?

Want to get on your favorite sports team with no added effort? Too good to be true. Work from home and make thousands per week? Until Covid, that was too good to be true. Trying to lose weight with this little pill / shake / extract — no exercise needed. Too good to be true.

Perhaps you invested your money for a guaranteed, large return, risk free. Run away fast — it is definitely too good to be true.

As we listen to Jesus here, I can't help but think: this sounds too good to be true.

Does Jesus mean that all we have to do is feed the hungry, welcome the lonely, clothe those who need it, and that is all he wants from us? Most of us in the church are doing that already, in some form. We do it through hands-on work and caring for our neighbors. We do it through giving our financial gifts. We're already there. Jesus should be happy. We can go home and relax, right?

* * *

Again, though, it's too good to be true.

The frame for this story started with Jesus saying, "The kingdom of heaven will be like this…"

People listening to him would have known that, in the ancient world, farmers separated sheep and goats for the night. Sheep, with their woolly coats, could stay outside. Goats needed to go inside. Jesus used that image to talk about sorting out people.

The story said that when the Son of Man — Jesus — comes in glory, all the nations will gather in front of him. The word translated as "nations" in our Bible is "*ethnoi*" in the original language. This is the same root of our word "ethnic." It can also be translated as Gentiles. Every time Matthew used this word, he meant the Gentiles — the outsiders. The outsiders were gathered in front of Jesus, too. Wait, how did they get there?

Interestingly, as Jesus told the story, both groups of people were clueless. Neither one saw Jesus in the people they met. Neither group knew what they had done.

* * *

Typically, we understand that the king in the story, dispensing judgment, is Jesus. But Jesus himself clearly told us where to find him in the story. We find him in the lost, the sick, the imprisoned, and the hungry.

The message of this parable is to worry less about judgment at the end of time and worry more about the people in front of us, because that's where we'll see Jesus. We find his face in the people who are battling an addiction, the people who struggle to find a job, the people who have chemo and radiation. We find Jesus in the kid who's being bullied, and in the trans kids who are finding their true selves. We find him in the struggles of people who are poor, or who feel like this country has forgotten them. We find him in the immigrants, making a new life in this country.

And, if that's us, we have a gift to give.

We know what it's like to be looked down on or overlooked. We know how to notice the people on the edges, the people on the outside.

* * *

This unity is part of what Jesus sought for all of us.

Author Melissa Florer-Bixler said that when we are called into the realm of God, this place is designed for everyone's blessedness. God is never done working on us. She writes, "As long as there are victims, there are victimizers. As long as there are oppressors, they will act on the oppressed. Our struggles are intertwined." When we see that, then "the good news has found its way to us." (from *How to Have An Enemy*) We announce the reign of God by knowing that the sheep and the goats are all part of the same whole.

* * *

Some years ago, when I lived in Washington, DC, after college, I usually went to the Presbyterian Church in the morning. Some weeks that wasn't enough, and I would join some friends for the casual Catholic mass at the end of the day on Sunday. It was low key, and jeans and a sweater were good enough for this evening mass.

One week, I met my friends there, and then the organizer of the mass came over to talk to them. He looked at me, and I got nervous. Was I doing something wrong? Was I going to be told to leave? My friends nodded, and the organizer came over to me.

He asked me, an ill-dressed random guest, if I would bring up the gifts when it was time for the sacrament of communion. Would I be willing to carry the bread and the cup up to the altar?

It's a moment of hospitality that I've never forgotten.

They didn't have to invite me, or even notice me, and yet their invitation assured me that I belonged there, in this version of the presence of God. I've never forgotten how special that felt, to move from the outside of the circle to the inside.

* * *

Still, before we get too excited about ourselves, notice that the righteous don't earn the realm of God, they inherit it. An inheritance comes because we're part of the family. As part of the family of faith, we care for each other without adding up the cost or keeping track. We notice each other, and what people need, as part of our everyday way of seeing the world.

Pastor Steve Garnaas-Holmes says that until we know what kind of ruler Jesus is, we can't see the realm of God. "Until we see the throne of the holy one rightly we see nothing. It's an upturned five-gallon bucket on a street corner, a bed in the locked ward, a cot in a refugee camp. A cell. A wheelchair. This is where the mystery abides. The burning sun of life, the hand that spins the universe, the uncontainable heart of grace, will not be confined to the familiar, the comfortable, the esteemed." (from *unfoldingLight.com*)

* * *

The people of God are waiting for us, wherever we go. Each one of them belongs to God, and we do, too, in the mysterious joining of all people in the heart of God. And there's Jesus in the midst of it all, changing our world into the world of God, bit by bit, day by day, action by action. In every moment of love, the reign of Christ comes closer.

May we join in, with all that we are and all that we have.

In the name of Jesus, a most unusual ruler, Amen.

Gross People Rule Thanksgiving

At Thanksgiving time, it's easy to do what the holiday commands, and find some things to be thankful for. Small or large, we all have something. A warm house, food in the fridge, older friends, younger friends. Good health, if we're fortunate enough to have that. Work we enjoy, if we're really fortunate. The blessing of retirement.

In tough seasons of life, we have to look harder. Even tiny things prompt our gratitude. The swoop of a bird outside the window, or the way nature paints a sunrise and a sunset — the comfort of our slippers — hot tea or coffee.

But after the Thanksgiving holiday is over, how do we make gratitude more than a one-day event?

There's lots of literature about how living with gratitude makes us happier and healthier, plus nicer to be around. We should be more grateful, and yet it slips away from us.

As we think about a life of gratitude, we have this person in the story as an example to ponder. We have to wonder, on this day especially, what made this one man turn back around, once he was healed? Did his aunties or his grandmother, his mother or stepmother, the women in his faith community — did they teach him this habit of giving thanks? He gave thanks to God, and then knelt — more than knelt — at Jesus' feet, overwhelmed by gratitude.

* * *

The other people healed by Jesus were doing exactly what Jesus told them to do.

The law required anyone who had been healed to go the priest, who would examine them, make sure they aren't contagious anymore, and then pronounce them clean. Then they could worship, live at home again, work, and be enfolded back into the community. Life didn't start again until the priest said so. Knowing this, Jesus sent them off, and, the story says, as they went, they were made clean.

So why was he so cranky about it, if they were doing exactly what he told them to do?

And, really, this one man could be complaining bitterly.

The story said that this man was a Samaritan, telling us without saying it that the others were Jews. When they were all sick, they had each other. They were all outcasts. They travelled together, joined by their misfortune. No one was noticing that he was a Samarian outcast because they all had to live outside the city, they all had to beg for food, they all had to avoid people.

When they're all lepers, they have each other. Once everyone was healed, their lives changed, and this man was left alone. This healing, that looks like such a gift, leaves this one man without his friends. He's not going to the priests because he's not going to be welcome there.

* * *

You've had that moment, too, I'll bet, when there's nowhere to go.

The chronic pain persists, or the marriage is over. Your child is suffering, and there's nothing you can do until they learn a lesson on their own. Or it's the time when your addiction has made a mess of your life, beyond your ability to fix it. It may be the moment when the doctor tells you that you have AIDS, cancer, or schizophrenia. When you see that pornography or gambling has taken over your life. The day when you lose your job or your house. The morning after someone you love dies, and grief overtakes you. The time when the person you love raises their hand to you, and you have an awful choice to make.

Now what?

John Kralik is someone who came to that same empty place. As he remembers it, [from DailyGood.org] on one New Year's Day, he was desperately looking for something, anything, for which to be thankful, he went for a walk to think. He owned a law practice, and realized that, after working all year, he hadn't actually made any money. He couldn't afford Christmas bonuses for his employees, which was embarrassing. The law firm was losing its lease, and he couldn't afford new office space. A divorce left him living in a cheap apartment. Everything felt hopeless, empty, worthless.

Then, he says, he heard a voice he did not recognize. "Wherever it came from, it did not seem to come from me. It told me I needed to learn to be grateful for the things I had, rather than to focus on the things I wanted, or the many things I felt I had lost."

To learn to be grateful, Kralik set out to write a thank you note every day for year. He quickly exhausted his list of family and co-workers, and had to dig deeply into his life, to really look around and notice things he had missed.

As he said, by the time he had written the 365 thank you notes he had set out to write, "my life had been transformed in ways I could not have expected. As I saw how my children, friends, coworkers, acquaintances, and even baristas [at the local coffee shop] had blessed my life and as I acknowledged their impact by writing to them, my blessings seemed to multiply. When I was grateful for clients paying their bills, they paid faster. When I thanked lawyers for referring clients to me, they referred more."

Gratitude turned him inside out.

Like the leper, who came back to Jesus in gratitude, John Kralik said, "Almost without intending to do so, I started to change my life in ways that would make me more worthy of receiving thank you notes myself."

The practice of noticing his life, pausing to be grateful, and then writing it down, changed him. He added: "Gratitude is a pathway to the peace that we all seek in life, the peace which passes our understanding. I still feel calmed in my dark or stressful times by writing "thank you" patiently and neatly to those who have helped and comforted me."

* * *

Giving thanks is the exit ramp from selfishness, and from discouragement. It lifts us out of the spiritual ill health that can take over our souls. It turns us back to the giver, just like the leper turned back to the giver of his new health. We all have times when there's nowhere to go, nothing we can do on our own, nothing within us that can help. We turn to the power outside ourselves, turn in need and gratitude.

And, of course, if you have more than the ordinary bleak spots in life, if the despair won't lift, see someone about it. God gave us counselors and medication as gifts, too.

* * *

The first part of the story is about the physical healing — all ten lepers were healed from the physical disease of leprosy. But the tenth had a second, added experience. When he came back, Jesus told him to go, "Your faith has made you well." This man's soul was touched, too. Something inside — as well as outside — changed for him. In this place where he had nowhere else to go, he saw what the others missed. In that empty place, he saw that he was in the presence of divine love and power, and he turned back.

In the same way, God comes into our emptiest places, too.

If the start of the holiday season is happy for you, give thanks with enthusiasm.

If the start of the holiday season is hard for you, if you feel empty and more alone than you want to be, if it's hard to find anything to be grateful for, squeeze out a small amount of gratitude, and then rest in God's care.

We turn toward God, in both need and gratitude, and God works to make us whole, too. We come into the deepest and best places of connection with the holy one, and with the holy within.

With thanksgiving to our generous God, Amen.

www.ingramcontent.com/pod-product-compliance
Lightning Source LLC
LaVergne TN
LVHW091207080426
835509LV00006B/876